West Virginia

BY HOLLY SAARI

Published by The Child's World®
1980 Lookout Drive • Mankato, MN 56003-1705
800-599-READ • www.childsworld.com

ACKNOWLEDGMENTS
The Child's World®: Mary Berendes, Publishing Director
The Design Lab: Design and production
Red Line Editorial: Editorial direction

PHOTO CREDITS: Sandra Calderbank/iStockphoto, cover, 1, 3; Matt
Kania/Map Hero, Inc., 4, 5; James Lemass/Photolibrary, 7; Stewart West/
iStockphoto, 9; iStockphoto, 10; Donald Erickson/iStockphoto, 11; David
Olah/iStockphoto, 13; North Wind Picture Archives/Photolibrary, 15; Pat
Canova/Photolibrary, 17; AP Images, 19; David Olah/iStockphoto, 21; One
Mile Up, 22; Quarter-dollar coin image from the United States Mint, 22

LIBRARY OF CONGRESS CATALOGING-IN-PUBLICATION DATA
Saari, Holly.
  West Virginia / by Holly Saari.
       p. cm.
  Includes bibliographical references and index.
  ISBN 978-1-60253-494-0 (library bound : alk. paper)
  1. West Virginia—Juvenile literature. I. Title.

F241.3.S23 2010
975.4—dc22

                         2010019914

Printed in the United States of America in Mankato, Minnesota.
July 2010
F11538

On the cover:
The Appalachian
Mountains run
through West
Virginia.

CONTENTS

Geography

Let's explore West Virginia! West Virginia is in the east-central United States. However, it is considered part of the South.

PENNSYLVANIA

OHIO

MARYLAND

• Wheeling

• Moundsville

Ohio River

• Fairmont

Berkeley
Springs

• Parkersburg

Clarksburg •

Kanawha River

• Elkins

WEST VIRGINIA

Appalachian Mountains

Huntington •

⭐ **Charleston**

• Fayetteville

VIRGINIA

Beckley •

White Sulphur Springs •

KENTUCKY

• Welch

NORTH

WEST   EAST

SOUTH

Cities

Charleston is the capital of West Virginia. It is the largest city in the state. Other large cities are Wheeling, Parkersburg, and Huntington.

Charleston is located on the Kanawha River. ▶

Land

West Virginia has mountains in the eastern and central parts of the state. They are part of the Appalachian Mountain Range. **Valleys** lie between the mountains. The west has a high, flat-topped surface called a **plateau**. The state has many rivers. The western border of the state is the Ohio River.

Rivers, mountains, and valleys make up ▶
much of West Virginia's landscape.

West Virginia is nicknamed "the Mountain State."

Plants and Animals

Forests cover most of West Virginia. Many animals live in the forests. These include deer and birds. The state tree is the sugar maple. The **sap** from this tree is used to make maple syrup. The state animal is the black bear. The state bird is the cardinal. Male cardinals are bright red. Females are often brown and red. The state flower is the rhododendron.

Maple trees turn beautiful colors in the fall. ▶

People and Work

About 1.8 million people live in West Virginia. Most of them live in **rural** areas. Many people in the state have jobs in **tourism**. Others work in **manufacturing**. They make **chemicals**, metal products, and paper products. Coal mining is also an important job.

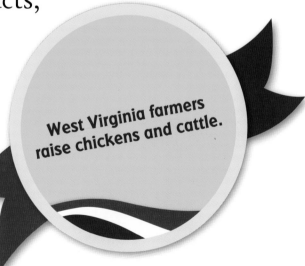

West Virginia farmers raise chickens and cattle.

West Virginia is known for coal mining. ▶

History

Native Americans have lived in the West Virginia area for thousands of years. People from Europe came to the area in the 1700s. On June 25, 1788, the West Virginia area entered the United States as part of Virginia. On June 20, 1863, West Virginia separated from Virginia. It became the thirty-fifth state.

Settlers built cabins near the Appalachian Mountains in West Virginia. ▶

West Virginia split into a new state because of an argument. In Virginia, easterners and westerners argued about slavery. Westerners did not want slavery. So they formed their own state.

15

Ways of Life

West Virginia is known for its beautiful nature. Many people come to the state to fish, hunt, and boat on its rivers. Visitors can camp in West Virginia's state parks.

Many people enjoy water activities in West Virginia. ▶

Famous People

Author Pearl S. Buck was born in West Virginia. She won an important prize for her writing. Gymnast Mary Lou Retton was born here, too. She won gold, silver, and bronze medals at the 1984 Olympics.

Mary Lou Retton was born in Fairmont. ▶

Famous Places

The West Virginia State **Museum** in Charleston is a **popular** place. Visitors can learn the history of coal mining and how the state was created. The city also has old homes that are popular to see.

Visitors to West Virginia can see historic sites with old log cabins. ▶

State Symbols

Seal

A miner and a farmer are on West Virginia's state seal. In front of them are **rifles**. The rifles stand for freedom. Go to childsworld.com/links for a link to West Virginia's state Web site, where you can get a firsthand look at the state seal.

Flag

West Virginia's flag has a colored state seal on it. It shows the rhododendron on the bottom.

Quarter

The state quarter shows the New River **Gorge**. It is a popular site to visit in West Virginia. The quarter came out in 2005.

Glossary

chemicals (KEM-uh-kulz): Chemicals are substances used in chemistry. Some people in West Virginia work to make chemicals.

gorge (GORJ): A gorge is a steep, narrow canyon. The New River Gorge is in West Virginia.

manufacturing (man-yuh-FAK-chur-ing): Manufacturing is the task of making items with machines. Manufacturing is important in West Virginia.

museum (myoo-ZEE-um): A museum is a place where people go to see art, history, or science displays. Charleston is home to a famous museum.

plateau (pla-TOH): A plateau is a flat area on the top of a hill or mountain. West Virginia has a plateau in the western part of the state.

popular (POP-yuh-lur): To be popular is to be enjoyed by many people. Outdoor activities are popular in West Virginia.

rifles (RYE-fulz): Rifles are long guns that are held up to the shoulder when fired. Rifles appear on West Virginia's state seal.

rural (ROOR-ul): Rural means having to do with the countryside. Most of the people in West Virginia live in rural areas.

sap (SAP): Sap is the liquid inside a plant or tree. The sap from West Virginia's sugar maple trees is made into maple syrup.

seal (SEEL): A seal is a symbol a state uses for government business. West Virginia's seal shows a miner and a farmer.

slavery (SLAYV-ur-ee): Slavery is the act of owning a person as property, forcing him or her to do work, and often treating that person badly. West Virginia split from Virginia because of an argument about slavery.

symbols (SIM-bulz): Symbols are pictures or things that stand for something else. The seal and the flag are West Virginia's symbols.

tourism (TOOR-ih-zum): Tourism is visiting another place (such as a state or country) for fun or the jobs that help these visitors. Tourism is popular in West Virginia.

valleys (VAL-eez): Valleys are the low points between two mountains. West Virginia has valleys.

Further Information

Books

Keller, Laurie. *The Scrambled States of America*. New York: Henry Holt, 2002.

Riehle, Mary Ann McCabe. *M is for Mountain State: A West Virginia Alphabet*. Chelsea, MI: Sleeping Bear Press, 2004.

Thornton, Brian. *The Everything Kids' States Book: Wind Your Way Across Our Great Nation*. Avon, MA: Adams Media, 2007.

Web Sites

Visit our Web site for links about West Virginia: *childsworld.com/links*

Note to Parents, Teachers, and Librarians: We routinely verify our Web links to make sure they are safe and active sites. So encourage your readers to check them out!

Index